The main tour takes about two hours. It starts and ends at Leeds Parish Church, where some street parking is available (max. 2 hours Monday - Saturday). The East End extension (Nos. 17 to 20) adds about 45 minutes to the main tour.

THE WALK

1 Leeds Parish Church. For more than a thousand years a church has stood on this site but when Dr W.D. Hook was appointed Vicar of Leeds in 1837, the medieval building was in a sorry state with congregations averaging around fifty worshippers. Believing 'a handsome church to be a kind of standing sermon', Hook along with his architect, R.D. Chantrell, produced a landmark building in the development of the Gothic Revival, deliberately aiming to reproduce an early 14th century church according to a proper Gothic plan.

This m
room
parish

GW00890424

All thi.....

and when the young Florence Nightingale attended the consecration she was shocked by the lighted candles on the altar and the vicar's 'regular Catholic jerk' when genuflecting before the altar. The interior of the church is well worth visiting: not only does it contain many monuments from the old church but the Victorian fittings and decoration (all cusps and crockets) are splendid, especially when one realises the tight budget that Chantrell was working to. Apart from wanting an impressive church, Hook wanted a large church with lots of free places - this was the beginning of his counter-attack against Methodism. In total the church cost £26,000 and had seating

Open during the day with refreshments and guidebook available.

for 3,000. Funds were difficult to raise at the onset of 'the Hungry Forties' and Chantrell had to exercise the strictest economy: stones and slates were re-used from the old church, much of what appears to be carved stone is in reality plaster, whilst cast iron is painted to look like oak. Even papier maché mixed with plaster was employed for some of the decorative detailing. Despite these constraints, the over-all effect is one of magnificence and the stunning view from the western gallery (if open) is well worth the effort of climbing the stairs at the back of the church.

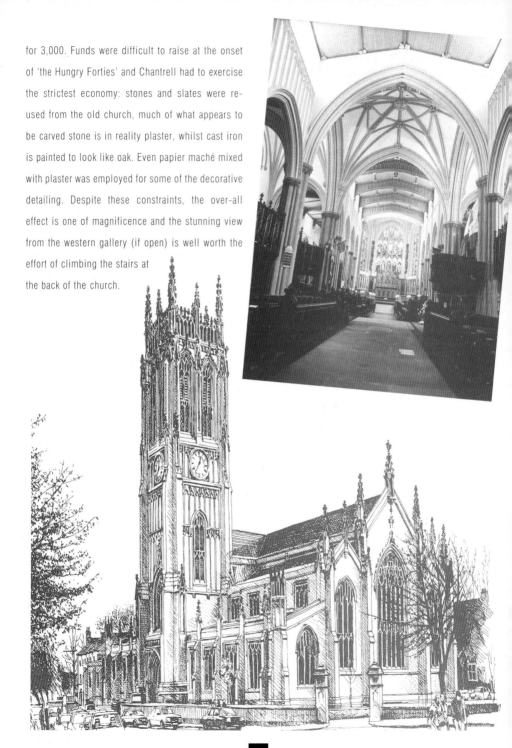

Walk up Kirkgate, turning right just before the railway viaduct into Cross York Street.

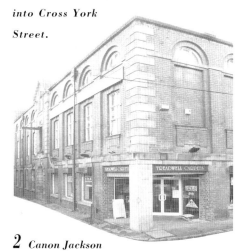

2 Canon Jackson Memorial Sunday School

The work of Sydney Kitson, youngest son of Sir James Kitson, the dominant feature of this example of Edwardian classicism is its facade with the lavish stonework of the pediment and prominent quoins -

best viewed form Back York Street. Canon Jackson was the d i s t i n g u i s h e d incumbent of St. James' church which until the 1950's stood adjacent, facing York Street. An octagonal building, St. James was built in 1794 as Zion Chapel for the New Connexion (a dissenting sect influenced by John Wesley) but was sold a year later to two Anglican clerics and incorporated into the Church of England in 1801.

Return to Kirkgate and cross over into Wharf Street, where you will find the Leeds Civic Trust Heritage Centre (open weekday mornings). At the end turn left into High Court and cross the main road to High Court Lane, which leads you to The Calls and Centenary Bridge (1993) with Tetley's Visitor Centre on the far side. The street names here refer to the medieval manor court of Leeds Kirkgate cum Holbeck which Ralph Paynel presented to the priors of Holy Trinity, York, in 1089.

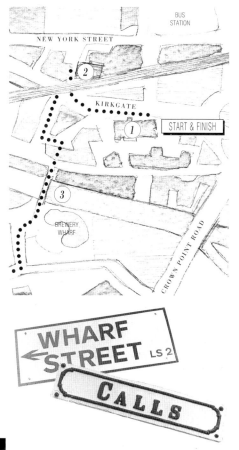

3 *View from Centenary Bridge*

From the bridge we catch a glimpse of three Leeds churches. To the east we can see the black outline of St. Saviour's, Richmond Hill (20). To the west rising above shops and offices of Briggate is the elegant silhouette of the tower of Holy Trinity (5), our next but one destination. Go to the far end of the bridge and looking again to the east, you can see the roof of Mount St. Mary's (19).

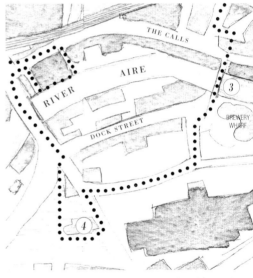

Go ahead with Brewery Wharf on the left and the Tetley Brewery complex in front. Turn left and then right on Waterloo Street. This leads into Hunslet Road. Across the road to the left are the buildings of Salem United Reform Church. Walk past the buildings and turn right down to the bottom of Salem Place to view the front of the church.

4 Salem Chapel

A Congregational chapel was erected here in 1791. A classical building with a pediment, the original chapel is now submerged in the rebuilding of 1907 which produced the distinctive curved frontage. At a time when most Non-Conformists favoured the gothic style, Salem preferred to maintain the austerity of the neo-classical. The windows of the original chapel can still be seen in Salem Place.

To the right of the church is a Sunday School in an Italianate style, added in the 1860s. The survival of Salem in a largely industrialised part of town was due to the pioneering joint ministry of Smith and Wrigley. In the first decades of the 19th century the worshippers had arrived in 'carriage and pair' but as early as 1841 many of them had left for the more salubrious East Parade Chapel. In 1888 the Chapel Council recommended closure but Smith and Wrigley were to breathe new life into the chapel with a mission which stressed the social message of the Gospels and fostered a new sense of community. A wide range of chapel activities were accommodated in a purpose built Institute erected in 1907.

Opposite the front of Salem until recently stood the Wesley Chapel of 1814. Water Lane just south of Leeds Bridge was the site of the Quaker Meeting House built in 1699.

Walk towards Leeds Bridge from which one can see the 43m tower of the Parish Church on the right. Once over the bridge turn right into The Calls and right again into Pitfall Street. Walk along the river bank past the new flats

On the north bank of the river just opposite the new flats of Riverside Court (built on the remains of the Aire Calder Navigation of 1824) is a single storey stone building, once part of a row of dock workers cottages, used as a dockside chapel for canal workers in the 1870s. In medieval times, at the north-east end of the bridge stood the chantry chapel of St. Mary on the Bridge.

Walk up Riverside Court, turn left into The Calls and then right into Briggate. Continue up Briggate, immediately after passing under the railway viaduct on the left, is Commercial Court.

Here in June 1842 the first Jewish wedding in Leeds was celebrated when Abigail, the daughter of Gabriel Davis, owner of a an optical instrument shop in Boar Lane, married James Cohen Pirani. It was Davis who in the late 1830s purchased a plot of land for £2 from the Earl of Cardigan for the Jewish cemetery in Gelderd Road, Gildersome which is still in use today. Cross over Briggate and Duncan Street to read the small plaque attached to the Yorkshire Building Society offices by the entrance to Hepworth Chambers. Here was the barber's shop of William Shent whose premises housed the first Methodist meetings in Leeds in the 1740s.

Cross Briggate and walk along Boar Lane.

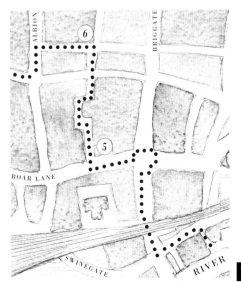

5 *Holy Trinity*

(open weekdays 8.30 am - 4 pm & occasional Saturdays, guidebook available)

By the beginning of the 18th century a group of wealthy merchants had emerged in Leeds who sought a social exclusivity not provided by the town's two existing churches. In 1721 they persuaded Lady Betty Hastings to contribute half the cost of a new church and the rest was to be raised by subscription. Holy Trinity became what is called a proprietary church because none of its places was open to the general public. Built in the form of a Roman basilica but always hemmed in by surrounding buildings, the main features its elegant exterior are on the southern elevation where a symmetrical frontage has balancing doors at either end (the eastern one is a sham) with Doric pilasters between, supporting a solid balustrade with urns.

The tower is not original but was designed by RD Chantrell in 1839. The interior is all space and light. Huge Corinthian columns support a moulded ceiling which to the east has the

appearance of a half dome (a real dome would have added considerably to the expense). Below, the splendid Venetian window is a gilded pelican, an ancient symbol of Christ's sacrifice.

Turn right by C & A into Trinity Street and go up the ramp and then diagonally across the square to reach the covered arcade by the Body shop. Turn right and then left out of the arcade by Marks and Spencer. Proceed north to reach the corner of Lands Lane and the Church Institute.

6 *The former Leeds Church Institute and Sunday Schools Association*

This impressive Gothic building recently cleaned and converted, was built by Adams and Kelly in 1866-7.

The Church Institute was founded by Dr Hook in the late 1840s to spearhead the Church of England's offensive against Non-Conformity and secularism. It once housed a lecture hall, reading room and library and as well as more conventional religious activities provided classes in English, Maths, French and Literature. The hub of much Anglican activity in the town, the building sheltered a wide array of organisations including the Missionary League and the Church Extension Society founded in 1865 to help finance the building of Anglican churches in the fast-growing suburbs of Leeds.

Walk up Albion Place towards West Riding House and turn left into Albion Street, first right into Bond Street and then second left down Park Row 100 metres to Mill Hill Chapel.

MILL HILL CHAPEL
This elegant Gothic building, designed by Bowman and Crowther in 1848, replaced the original 17th century chapel. Its congregation—formerly Presbyterian, now Unitarian—dates from 1672. Joseph Priestley, LL.D., F.R.S., discoverer of oxygen, was minister here 1767 — 1773.

7 Mill Hill Unitarian Chapel
(open Saturdays 10am - 12 noon)

The present chapel stands on the site of the first dissenting meeting house in Leeds built in 1672 on what was then the edge of the township. Joseph Priestley, the discoverer of oxygen, was minister here between 1767-73 and his statue can be seen opposite in City Square. The original building survived until the 1840s, when the wealthy congregation decided to rebuild in a style which would 'be more creditable to our taste hereafter'. An early example of the Non-Conformist use of a correct Gothic plan and style, the design bears an uncanny resemblance to the Parish Church - all that is missing is the tower! Some sections of Anglican opinion were outraged as they felt they had proprietary rights over this style. Criticism also came from Non-Conformist quarters which regarded the use of this design as something of a 'sell-out' to the Established Church. The interior is as 'churchy' as its exterior, with a magnificent stone pulpit, a reredos and lots of stained glass, some by William Morris.

Walk up Park Row to the Headrow. Cross the Headrow and turn left, past the Town Hall to Oxford Place.

OXFORD PLACE

Before looking at the front of the chapel, go to the rear where you can see a typically plain Non-Conformist chapel of the early 19th century. It was designed in 1835 by James Simpson with seating for 2,250. The lavish new front facade and extensions were added between 1896-1903. This Baroque style is an unusual one for Leeds and includes a tall campanile with an open lantern tower - something more readily associated with continental Roman Catholic churches.

Walk up Oxford Place. Turn left along Great George Street. Beyond the Leeds General Infirmary is St. George's Church.

By the 1830s Little Woodhouse was becoming a suburban retreat for the wealthy of Leeds eager to escape the dirt and the noise of the town. St. George's was built between 1836-8 to serve their spiritual needs. The architect was the town's leading classicist, John Clarke, and although some of the detailing here is Gothic (see the tall lancet windows), the over-all plan is not. Not only did the church initially lack a chancel but instead of an east window there was a huge Renaissance style painting by C W Cope RA, a native of Leeds and friend of John Atkinson, the owner of Little Woodhouse Hall and the pioneer of the suburban development here. The tower at the west end once carried a spire but this was damaged in a storm in 1962 and had to be removed. The octagonal sanctuary apse is an addition of 1898-99. Large burial vaults were incorporated into the original plan. Closed since 1855 on public health grounds, they were re-opened in 1930 by the vicar, Don Robins, to provide a sanctuary for the unemployed.

GREAT GEORGE ST

Return along Great George Street behind the Town Hall. Cross Calverley Street and continue to the junction of Great George Street and Cookridge Street to reach St. Anne's.

10 *St. Anne's Roman Catholic Cathedral* (open daily, guidebook available).

The first St. Anne's church faced out onto the Headrow, blocking what was later to become Cookridge Street. It was built in 1838 by John Child and raised to cathedral status in 1878. By the end of the century in order to improve traffic flow, the City Council compulsorily purchased the site and provided the present location with £46,000 compensation.

The architects of the new church were the London-based J H Eastwood and S E Greenslade who had to meet the challenge of this awkward, virtually square site.

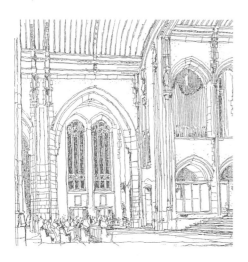

This explains St. Anne's unconventional plan particularly the short but extremely broad nave. By 1900, the Gothic passion was waning and here is blended with the simpler, freer Art and Crafts style. The west front was designed as the main entrance and has more decorative detail than any other section of the exterior. The interior is spacious and simple with what has been described as 'a boat-shaped roof'. Not to be missed is the jewel-like reredos by AWN Pugin, originally the high altar of the old church but now standing in the Lady Chapel to the SE.

Continue up Great George Street pausing to admire Cathedral House,

the Art and Crafts clergy house also by Eastwood and Greenslade. Turn left into Woodhouse Lane, and beyond what was once the City of Leeds School (now the Benefits Advice Centre) lies a group of chapel buildings now used by Leeds Metropolitan University and the Leeds College of Music.

11 *Woodhouse Lane Methodist New Connexion Chapel and Schools.*

New Connexion Methodism originated in Leeds in 1798 as a protest against the loss of power by lay members of the church.

Their first chapel was off Vicar Lane and they moved here in 1858. This classical building was designed by William Hill, a member of the chapel and one-time assistant to Cuthbert Brodrick, the architect of the Town Hall. The school premises next door were erected to Hill's designs in 1888. The most well-known member of the congregation was Henry Marsden. Born in the slums of Holbeck, he amassed a fortune in the USA and returned to Leeds in 1860, thirteen years later becoming the town's mayor. His statue financed by public subscription, once stood near the chapel but now can be found on Woodhouse Moor. The chapel was closed in 1928.

Cross Woodhouse Lane and go north to turn right at the traffic lights and then cross Claypit Lane opposite the public house (alternatively Woodhouse Lane may be crossed by underpass at the traffic lights).

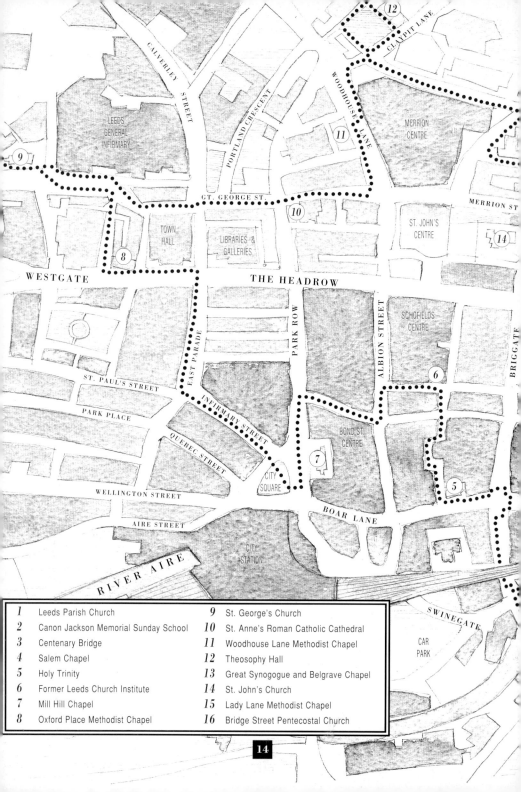

1   Leeds Parish Church
2   Canon Jackson Memorial Sunday School
3   Centenary Bridge
4   Salem Chapel
5   Holy Trinity
6   Former Leeds Church Institute
7   Mill Hill Chapel
8   Oxford Place Methodist Chapel
9   St. George's Church
10 St. Anne's Roman Catholic Cathedral
11 Woodhouse Lane Methodist Chapel
12 Theosophy Hall
13 Great Synogogue and Belgrave Chapel
14 St. John's Church
15 Lady Lane Methodist Chapel
16 Bridge Street Pentecostal Church

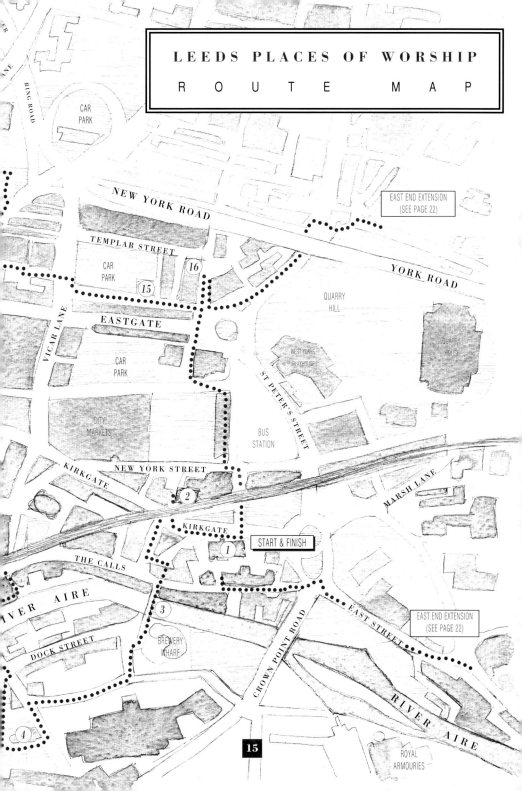

LEEDS PLACES OF WORSHIP
ROUTE MAP

CAR PARK

RING ROAD

NEW YORK ROAD

EAST END EXTENSION (SEE PAGE 22)

TEMPLAR STREET

CAR PARK

(16)

(15)

YORK ROAD

VICAR LANE

EASTGATE

QUARRY HILL

WEST YORKS PLAYHOUSE

QUARRY HOUSE

CAR PARK

CITY MARKETS

ST PETER'S STREET

BUS STATION

KIRKGATE

NEW YORK STREET

(2)

MARSH LANE

KIRKGATE

(1)

START & FINISH

THE CALLS

RIVER AIRE

(3)

CROWN POINT ROAD

EAST STREET

EAST END EXTENSION (SEE PAGE 22)

BREWERY WHARF

DOCK STREET

RIVER AIRE

(4)

ROYAL ARMOURIES

QUEEN SQUARE

Queen Square may be entered through a gap in the wall to the right of the pub. Walk round the square to reach Theosophy Hall.

12 *Theosophy Hall, 12 Queen Square*

By the end of the 19th century, not all spiritual needs were being met by orthodox religion. Theosophy, founded in 1875 by the colourful Madame Blavatsky, blended various Eastern traditions of thought and spirituality. The inaugural meeting of the Leeds Society was held in 1893 and the Hall was purchased in 1911. It was opened by Annie Besant, a socialist and early campaigner for Women's Rights - she was the leader of the legendary Match Girls Strike in 1888, but later became a leading Theosophist and champion of the cause of Indian Independence.

From Queen Square cross over Claypit Lane and go down Merrion Way to Wade Lane. At the bottom, where the Yorkshire Bank now stands, stood Brunswick Methodist Chapel, built 1824. All that now remains is the War Memorial and sections of perimeter wall. Walk towards the City Centre and take the second left into Belgrave Street.

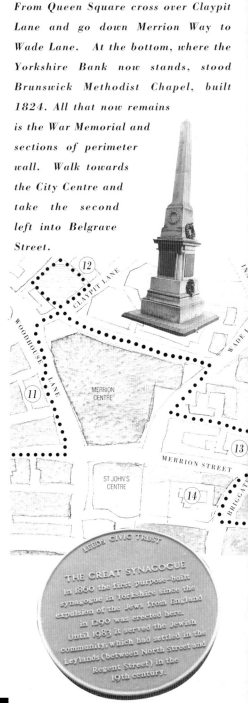

LEEDS CIVIC TRUST

THE GREAT SYNAGOGUE

In 1860 the first purpose-built synagogue in Yorkshire since the expulsion of the Jews from England in 1290 was erected here. Until 1983 it served the Jewish community, which had settled in the Leylands (between North Street and Regent Street) in the 19th century.

13 The Great Synagogue and Belgrave Chapel.

A blue Civic Trust plaque attached to the modern building on the left, marks the site of the first purpose-built synagogue in Leeds. Erected before the mass immigration of Russian and Eastern European Jews in the 1890s, these later immigrants always referred to the synagogue as 'the englisher shool' and built their own smaller 'grinner' (newcomer) places of worship amongst the houses and workshops of the crowded Leylands. Belgrave Hall which stands on the right at the bottom of Belgrave Street has been so splendidly refurbished that it is difficult to detect its origins as an austere Congregational chapel built in 1836. The growing respectability of Dissent in the course of the 19th century usually meant a shift in location from east and south to the northern parts of the town but Belgrave is an exception. An off-shoot of Albion Chapel (situated where the Bond St Centre now is), the chapel was intended as a missionary endeavour to 'the east-end'. Despite an opening sermon which committed the chapel to 'the gospel of salvation to be published to the ruined and the lost', only 500 of its 1800 places were free of pew rents!

At the end of Belgrave Street turn right. Cross over Merrion Street and Walk down New Briggate. St. John's is just before Lewis's

It is the interior which makes St. John's so noteworthy for here we find a church designed for a very different form of Anglican worship and with a virtually complete set of 17th century fittings.

JOHN HARRISON
1579-1656

St. John's, one of England's most remarkable churches, was built by this celebrated benefactor in 1634. A cloth merchant and co-founder of Leeds Corporation, he further endowed the town with almshouses, a new grammar school and a market cross.

As the oldest church in Leeds and one of national importance, it is difficult to believe that there were plans in the 1860s to demolish St. John's. We owe its survival to the intervention of the architect, Norman Shaw, who was in Leeds to supervise the building of Cookridge Hospital. Amazed by such an act of vandalism, Shaw wrote that St. John's represented 'a specimen of church architecture to which no other town I know in England can produce a parallel'. The church was founded in the 1630s by John Harrison, a Leeds woollen merchant. Often mistaken now as a building of the Victorian Gothic Revival, it is an example of Gothic surviving long after the end of the Middle Ages.

The plan of the church, with two parallel naves, is inconvenient for modern worship; but in John Harrison's time the focal point of the service was the pulpit, which once stood at the centre of the north wall, with pews facing it. Holy Communion was then regarded as a private rather than a public ceremony. It took place infrequently, and behind the chancel screen. The great glory of the church is its woodwork based on Flemish designs. The screen in particular is a masterpiece of delicate carving and its naturalism is echoed in the plaster panels of the ceiling. Look up at the corbels; robust angels above the nave, more elegant figures over the chancel, and strange hermaphrodites tucked away in corners. The tomb of the founder is in the chancel and the front pew still carries the iron holder in which as Chief Alderman he placed the town mace.

The stone building in the south-west corner of the grave yard stands on the site of the Leeds Charity School. A Civic Trust plaque gives details of the history of the present building.

Leave the church by the New Briggate gateway. Cross New Briggate and go down Harrison Street. Cross Vicar Lane, turn right and almost immediately left down Lady Lane.

15 Lady Lane Methodist Chapel

A classical chapel built in 1839-40 by James Simpson for the Wesleyan Methodist Association, a Methodist secession. Previously the site had been occupied by St. Mary's, the first Roman Catholic Church to be built in Leeds since the Reformation. Erected between 1792-4, at a time when it was still illegal for Catholic churches to have bell towers or steeples, St Mary's appeared indistinguishable from a dissenters meeting house. The church was closed in 1838 when the congregation moved to St Anne's.

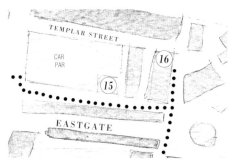

Continue to the bottom of Lady Lane and turn left into Bridge Street.

16 Bridge Street Pentecostal Church

TO THE GLORY OF GOD
THIS STONE WAS LAID BY
PRINCIPAL GEORGE JEFFREYS
(FOUNDER AND LEADER OF THE
ELIM FOURSQUARE GOSPEL ALLIANCE)
ON THE
1ST DAY OF NOVEMBER 1930

The most recent chapel to be constructed in the city centre. Built for the Elim Foursquare Gospel Alliance in 1930 in brick with faience dressings, the architectural style of the building would probably be termed Edwardian Free Style, an eclectic mixture of baroque and gothic features.

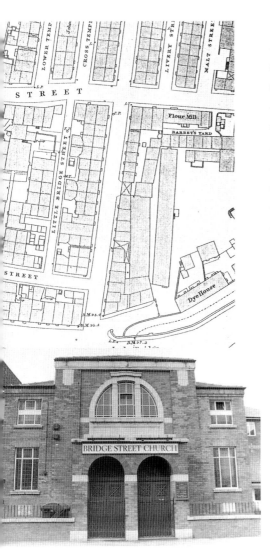

Return back down Bridge Street towards Eastgate roundabout. If you wish to take the Extension to the East End churches see the route directions on the next page. Otherwise cross over Eastgate and Union Street into Millgarth Street and turn left past the Police Station. Turn right and walk through the bus station (perhaps stopping for a well deserved cup of tea) and after emerging from the covered concourse cross over York Street and go down Church Lane under the Viaduct to reach the end of the walk at the Parish Church.

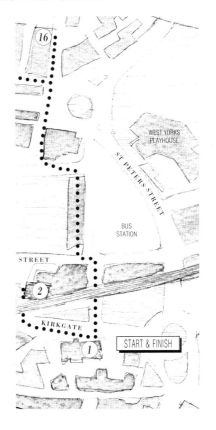

It was in a loft in Bridge Street that the handful of Jewish families (of German extraction) living in Leeds in the 1830s organised their first religious services. Lower down, beyond the bridge which carries New York Road over Bridge Street, stands the Leylands School, built in 1875. In 1888 Leeds School Board agreed that Hebrew classes could be given here after school hours.

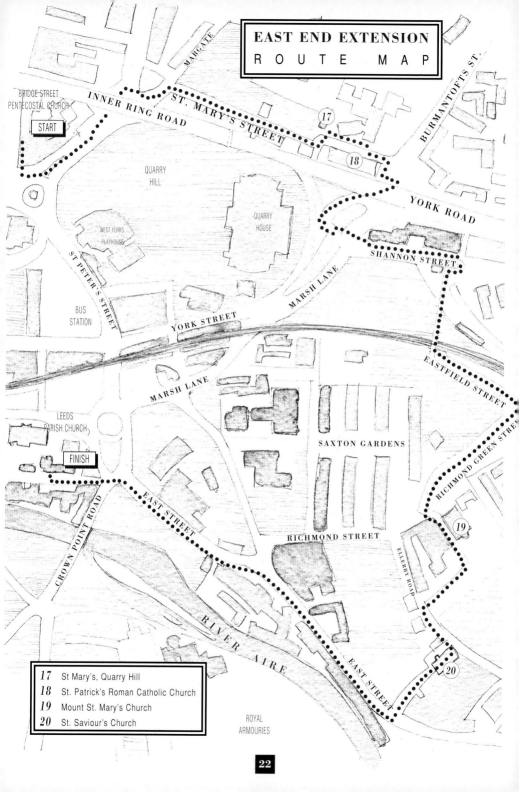

EAST END EXTENSION
R O U T E   M A P

BRIDGE STREET
PENTECOSTAL CHURCH
START

INNER RING ROAD

ST. MARY'S STREET

MARGATE

BURMANTOFTS ST.

17

18

YORK ROAD

QUARRY HILL

QUARRY HOUSE

WEST YORKS PLAYHOUSE

SHANNON STREET

ST PETER'S STREET

MARSH LANE

BUS STATION

YORK STREET

EASTFIELD STREET

MARSH LANE

LEEDS PARISH CHURCH

FINISH

SAXTON GARDENS

RICHMOND GREEN STREET

19

EAST STREET

RICHMOND STREET

ELLERBY ROAD

CROWN POINT ROAD

RIVER AIRE

EAST STREET

20

ROYAL ARMOURIES

17 St Mary's, Quarry Hill
18 St. Patrick's Roman Catholic Church
19 Mount St. Mary's Church
20 St. Saviour's Church

EAST END EXTENSION

You will be well rewarded if you have the time - it takes about 45 minutes - to extend your walk to take in the four East End churches. Alternatively you could make this a separate walk. From the Eastgate roundabout keep left and walk past the Job Centre and under the elevated New York Road. Cross Regent Street and go up St. Mary's Road between the grass banks, once the graveyard of St. Mary's, Quarry Hill.

17 St. Mary's, Quarry Hill

At the top of the hill, the stone walled enclosure on the left marks the site of the Parliamentary Church of St. Mary's, constructed in 1823 from the £1 million fund set aside by the Government in 1818 'to ensure the education of the poor in the principles of the Established Church'. All that now remains is the school designed by R D Chantrell in 1829.

Originally a single storeyed box-like building, its decoration was confined to plain arched windows and doorway for the sake of economy. A second storey was added in 1848 and the school-master's house which stands at the far end is a later addition of the 1860s.

Continue along Rider Street.

18 St. Patrick's Roman Catholic Church.

A 'neat and chaste' church was built here in 1831 to minister to the Irish immigrants who had been moving to Leeds ever since 1800. After years of weekly house-to-house collections, the working-class congregation was able to afford a new church in 1891, costing £11,000. Designed by the town's foremost Catholic architect, John Kelly, it is reminiscent of French or German churches with its cross-gabled aisles, blind arcading and treatment of its intricate roof spaces. The interior is dominated by an apsidal east end covered with wall paintings by Belgian artists.

From the York Road frontage of St. Patrick's Church, turn right and follow the footpath under the elevated New York Road to Quarry House. At Quarry House turn left and use the pedestrian route to cross Marsh Lane into Shannon Street. After 100 metres turn right up the ramp and cross the railway footbridge. At the end of the bridge, turn left up East Field Street and take the next right into Cross Catherine Street (a dirt road) which a little later becomes Church Road. Steps on the left will take you to Mount St. Mary's Church which we earlier glimpsed from Centenary Bridge (3).

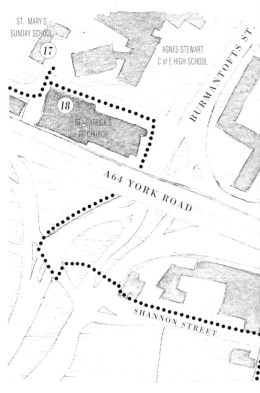

19 Mount St. Mary's Church.

This citadel-like complex giving fine views across the city contains St. Mary's church, convent, two schools and presbytery. Financed as a missionary endeavour by the French Order of the Oblates of Mary Immaculate, the massive and sumptuous church was built in 1853-7 to the designs of William Wardell and J.A. Hansom (of Hansom cab fame). The apsidal chancel and transepts added in 1866 were by E.W. Pugin, son of the more famous Gothic revivalist, A.N.W. Pugin. The vast interior has a moving grandeur but at the time of writing most of its splendid fittings have been removed, and the future of the church is uncertain.

Leave the church by the east end, turning right into Willis Street and take a left turn into Ellerby Road On the right is our final destination, St. Saviour's Church.

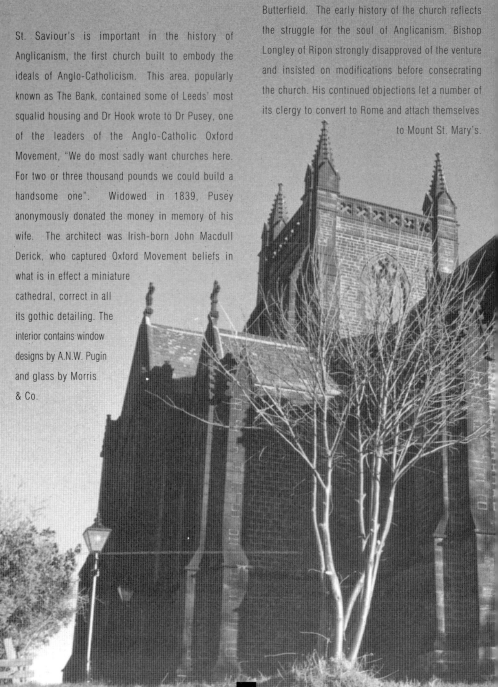

20 *St. Saviour's Church*

St. Saviour's is important in the history of Anglicanism, the first church built to embody the ideals of Anglo-Catholicism. This area, popularly known as The Bank, contained some of Leeds' most squalid housing and Dr Hook wrote to Dr Pusey, one of the leaders of the Anglo-Catholic Oxford Movement, "We do most sadly want churches here. For two or three thousand pounds we could build a handsome one". Widowed in 1839, Pusey anonymously donated the money in memory of his wife. The architect was Irish-born John Macdull Derick, who captured Oxford Movement beliefs in what is in effect a miniature cathedral, correct in all its gothic detailing. The interior contains window designs by A.N.W. Pugin and glass by Morris & Co.

The adjacent vicarage (1847) is by William Butterfield. The early history of the church reflects the struggle for the soul of Anglicanism. Bishop Longley of Ripon strongly disapproved of the venture and insisted on modifications before consecrating the church. His continued objections let a number of its clergy to convert to Rome and attach themselves to Mount St. Mary's.

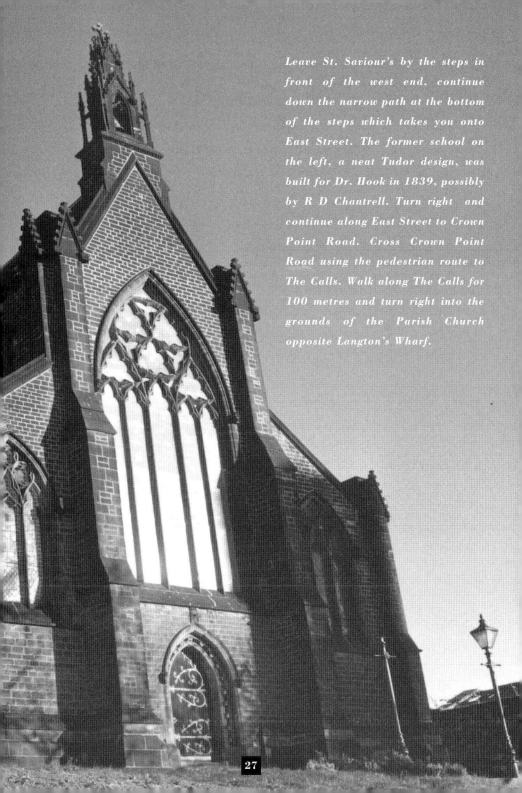

Leave St. Saviour's by the steps in front of the west end, continue down the narrow path at the bottom of the steps which takes you onto East Street. The former school on the left, a neat Tudor design, was built for Dr. Hook in 1839, possibly by R D Chantrell. Turn right and continue along East Street to Crown Point Road. Cross Crown Point Road using the pedestrian route to The Calls. Walk along The Calls for 100 metres and turn right into the grounds of the Parish Church opposite Langton's Wharf.

RELIGIOUS BUILDINGS OF PARTICULAR HISTORIC
OR ARCHITECTURAL INTEREST OUTSIDE THE CITY CENTRE

Friends Meeting House, New Adel Lane, Adel.

St. John the Baptist, Church Lane, Adel.

Primitive Methodist Chapel (now a warehouse), Stanningley Road/Branch Road, Armley.

St Bartholomew, Wesley Road, Armley.

Bramhope Chapel, Otley Road, Bramhope.

St. Matthew, Wood Lane, Chapel Allerton.

The New Synagogue (now a theatre), Chapeltown Road, Chapeltown.

Newton Park Union Church (now a Sikh Temple), Chapeltown Road, Chapeltown.

St. Chad, Otley Road, Far Headingley.

Epiphany, Foundry Lane, Gipton.

St. Wilfred, Selby Road, Halton.

St. Aidan, Roundhay Road, Harehills.

The Bilal Mosque, Harehills Lane, Harehills.

Christadelphian Hall, Brudenell Road, Headingley.

First Church of Christ Scientist (now a school) Headlingley Lane, Headingley.

Headingley Hill Congregational Chapel, Headingley Lane, Headingley.

Headingley Wesleyan Methodist Chapel, Otley Road, Headingley.

St. Michael, Headingley Lane, Headingley.

Wesley College, Headingley Lane, Headingley.

Prospect United Methodist Free Church (now a warehouse), Domestic Street, Holbeck.

St. Margaret, Church Lane, Horsforth.

Kirkstall Abbey, Abbey Road, Kirkstall.

Baptist Chapel (new offices), Meanwood Road, Meanwood.

St John, Wetherby Road, Roundhay.

The Synagogue of the United Hebrew Congregation, Shadwell Lane, Shadwell.

St Mary, Colton Road, Whitkirk.

Friends Meeting House (now Radio Leeds), Woodhouse Lane, Woodhouse.

All Souls, Blackman Lane, Woodhouse.

St. Mark, St Mark's Road, Woodhouse

The Hostel of the Resurrection (now part of the University), Springfield Mount, Woodhouse.